Great Escapes

Henry Billings

Melissa Stone

STECK-VAUGHN
COMPANY
ELEMENTARY • SECONDARY • ADULT • LIBRARY

Books in this series:
Great Disasters
Great Escapes
Great Mysteries
Great Rescues

Acknowledgments

Supervising Editor
Kathleen Fitzgibbon
Project Editor
Christine Boyd
Designer
Sharon Golden
Photo Editor
Margie Matejcik

Illustration Credits
Cover Illustration: Rhonda Childress

Gary McElhaney: pp. 36, 37, 38, 42, 43, 45, 47, 58, 59, 62
Jimmy Longacre: pp. 8, 9, 10, 13, 24, 25, 27, 30, 31, 33

Photo Credits
Pp. 2, 3 UPI/Bettmann Newsphotos; p. 4 The Bettmann Archive; pp. 16, 17 Culver Pictures, Inc.; p. 21 UPI/Bettmann Newsphotos; p. 50 Courtesy the National Park Service; p. 51 UPI/Bettmann Newsphotos; p. 53 UPI/Bettmann Newsphotos; p. 54 AP/Wide World; p. 55 © Bill Nation/Sygma; pp. 66, 67, 68, 69 AP/Wide World; p. 72 © Heggemann/Stern/Black Star; p. 73 both © Heggemann/Stern/Black Star; p. 75 © Stern/Black Star; p. 76 © Jahn/Stern/Black Star; pp. 80, 81, 83 AP/Wide World.

ISBN 0-8114-4177-6

7 8 9 10 PO 00 99 98 97

Contents

No Lock Could Hold Him

The police officer walked into the locksmith's shop. He brought with him a handcuffed prisoner.

"The lock on these cuffs is broken," the police officer said. "I need you to cut the cuffs off."

Erich Weiss tried to cut the cuffs, but the steel was too hard. Weiss later said, "I broke six saw blades. Then a thought struck me. Maybe I could pick the lock."

Weiss **succeeded.** In fact, he picked the lock so easily that he soon tried others. Weiss used his new skill to put together a magic act. And he gave himself a new name–Harry Houdini.

Houdini gets ready for another impossible escape.

An Amazing Act

Between 1895 and 1926, Houdini's act **stunned** the world. It seemed that he could escape from anything. No ropes or locks or chains could hold him. Houdini escaped from boxes, safes, and prison rooms.

In 1903, Houdini took his act to Russia. There he met Moscow's chief of police.

"Please lock me in your jail. I'd like to prove that I can escape from it," he said.

The chief had heard about Houdini's magic. He wanted no part in it. He turned Houdini down.

"How about the Carette, then?" Houdini asked.

The chief smiled. The Carette was a six-foot-square steel box. It was used to carry Russia's worst prisoners to Siberia. The Carette had two openings. One was a tiny window with bars. The other was a steel door. The chief could lock the door. But he could not unlock it. The key was 2,000 miles away in Siberia.

"No one has ever escaped from the Carette," the chief told Houdini.

Houdini smiled. "I'll get out," he said.

The chief made Houdini take off his clothes. He searched him for tools. He handcuffed Houdini and chained his legs together. Houdini climbed into the box, and the chief locked the door.

For the next 28 minutes, the chief waited. "He'll never get out," he thought.

But suddenly, Houdini appeared from behind the Carette. The door was still locked. The handcuffs and chains were also locked and lying on the floor. But somehow Houdini had escaped. No one ever found out how he did it.

Underwater

Back in America, Houdini came up with another great act. A large glass box was placed on the

Houdini is being strapped into a jacket.

stage. Houdini stood inside the box. A heavy piece of glass was lowered onto the box. The cover was locked on each side. Four tight straps passed over and under the box. Then water was poured into the box from a small hole in the top. Houdini was trapped. He had no way to reach the locks or straps. He had no way to breathe, either.

Houdini's helper pulled a curtain in front of the box. People in the crowd waited **anxiously.** No one, not even Houdini, could breathe underwater. In four or five minutes he would drown. As the minutes passed, people began to **panic.** They feared Houdini was dead.

Then, suddenly, the curtain was pulled back. There stood Houdini, dripping wet. Behind him was the glass box. It was still filled with water. Its locks and straps were still in place. Houdini smiled at the people in the crowd. He had tricked them again.

Buried Alive!

But Houdini didn't stop there. He came up with yet another trick. This time he climbed into a box that was **bolted** shut. The box was lowered six feet into the ground. The hole was filled with 3,000 pounds of sand.

The **audience** watched **fearfully.** Houdini was buried alive! He could never escape from the bolted box. And even if he did, he would be **crushed** by the heavy sand.

"He's going to die down there!" someone cried.

But all at once, the sand moved. A moment later, Houdini's curly head popped out of the sand. He had done it! Once again the great Houdini had **mysteriously** escaped **death.**

Do You Remember?

■ In the blank, write the letter of the best ending for each sentence.

_____ 1. Before opening his magic act, Houdini worked in a
   a. locksmith shop.   b. post office.   c. circus.

_____ 2. Houdini was the first person ever to escape from
   a. Russia.   b. the Carette.   c. jail.

_____ 3. The key to the Carette was kept in
   a. America.   b. Germany.   c. Siberia.

_____ 4. When Houdini came out of the glass box, he was
   a. soaking wet.   b. coughing.   c. sick.

_____ 5. Houdini found it easy to
   a. pick locks.   b. bend coins.   c. write books.

Express Yourself

■ Imagine that you are a reporter for a magazine. You have just seen Houdini escape from the glass box. Write an article about what you saw.

_____

_____

_____

_____

_____

_____

_____

Exploring Words

■ Read each sentence. Fill in the circle next to the best meaning for the word in dark print. If you need help, use the Glossary.

1. Houdini **succeeded** in getting out of the Carette.
   ○ a. was able to　　○ b. feared　　○ c. forgot

2. People were **stunned** by Houdini's act.
   ○ a. angered　　○ b. badly hurt　　○ c. surprised

3. People watched **anxiously** as Houdini was buried alive.
   ○ a. happily　　○ b. with cruel thoughts　　○ c. nervously

4. Houdini knew it was important not to **panic.**
   ○ a. become frightened　　○ b. cry　　○ c. shout loudly

5. The box was **bolted** before it was put in the ground.
   ○ a. painted　　○ b. opened　　○ c. locked with a bar

6. The **audience** was afraid Houdini would drown.
   ○ a. child　　○ b. people watching　　○ c. deaf person

7. People stared **fearfully** at the glass box.
   ○ a. with great hope　　○ b. with fear　　○ c. secretly

8. It seemed that Houdini would be **crushed** by the sand.
   ○ a. squeezed painfully　　○ b. lifted　　○ c. worried

9. Houdini smiled **mysteriously**.
   ○ a. hard to explain　　○ b. in a slow way　　○ c. easily

10. Houdini always managed to escape **death**.
    ○ a. disease　　○ b. the police　　○ c. the end of life

Running for the Border

Lieutenant John Donaldson was led forward by the German guard. Donaldson, an American, was angry. He didn't like being pushed around. Just a few hours earlier, he had been free. He had been up in his plane, flying a **combat mission.** With the mission completed, he had turned his plane around to go home. But the Germans had shot him down. Now, on September 1, 1918, he was a World War I prisoner of war.

The First Try

As soon as Donaldson got to his prison cell, he began planning an escape.

"There's got to be some way we can break out of here," he said to the 16 other prisoners.

The men shook their heads.

"It's too dangerous," said one. "It's impossible to get through the German **lines**. All you'll get for your trouble is a bullet in the back."

Donaldson thought the man was probably right. But his mind was set on escaping.

Three days later, the Germans brought in a new prisoner. He was an American pilot named Oscar Mandel. Mandel wanted to escape from the prison as much as Donaldson did. So the two men decided to work together.

At nine o'clock that same night, they jumped from the second-floor window of the prison. Then they sneaked out of the prison yard and into the night. They took with them a **compass,** a loaf of bread, and a map from an English newspaper.

"Now comes the hard part," Donaldson whispered to Mandel. "Somehow we have to get past the German lines."

For five days and nights the two men stumbled blindly behind German lines. They ran out of food. They grew cold and tired. Hunger knotted their stomachs. But they did not give up.

Luckily, Mandel spoke German perfectly. Because of this, they were able to make their way through the countryside.

By the sixth day, they were close to freedom. The English lines were right in front of them. But as they were crossing a stream, they were **spotted** and captured.

Donaldson and Mandel were prisoners again. But they were not taken back to the same prison. The guards there said Americans were a bad influence on the rest of the prisoners. Instead, the two men were sent to a different prison and were put in a little room over the guardroom.

A Second Breakout

Donaldson was **discouraged**. But he wasn't ready to give up. Sixteen days later, Mandel and Donaldson used a saw to cut a hole in the roof of their cell. Three other prisoners crawled through the hole with them. These men were called Andy, Tilly, and George.

The five men climbed down into the prison yard. They climbed up the prison wall and down the other side. Night after night, they crept through enemy land. They swam across rivers and climbed over fences. They hid in empty barns and old buildings. They crawled through mud and ate whatever roots and berries they could find. Many times farmers would give them food, shelter, or clothing.

After four days, the men made it into Belgium. Belgium was controlled by the Germans. If they could cross Belgium into Holland, they would be safe.

Then George spoke up. "I know a man who lives in Belgium. I'm sure he will help us!"

They made their way to the Belgian's town. Donaldson, Tilly, and Andy hid in a nearby forest. Mandel and George went into the town to find George's friend. For 24 hours, Donaldson and the other two waited. Finally, Donaldson said, "Something's gone wrong. We'll have to go on without them."

Andy and Tilly hated to leave without Mandel and George. But they knew Donaldson was right. They had to keep going. For the next few days they moved carefully toward the Holland **border**. German soldiers seemed to be everywhere. Yet somehow, the three men stayed hidden. Later, they learned that Mandel and George had been captured and returned to prison.

A Mad Dash for Freedom

At last they reached the border between Holland and Belgium. To get to Holland, they had to cross three **barbed** wire fences. The first one was an ordinary fence. So was the last one. But the middle one had five thousand **volts** of electricity running through it. That was enough electricity to kill anyone who touched it.

Donaldson knew they would have to cut through the electric fence. For several days he and the others sneaked around the border towns. They searched for a pair of wirecutters. At last they found some. On the night of October 23, they were finally ready to go. Andy put on rubber gloves and grabbed the wirecutters.

German guards walked back and forth in front of the fences. Each guarded an area of about 200 yards (about the length of two football fields). Donaldson knew that one of these guards might spot them. But he also knew that this was their chance for freedom.

They waited until the guard closest to them had passed and was about 100 yards away. Then they ran for the fences. They climbed through the first fence. Then they dropped onto their stomachs. Andy

reached out with the wirecutters. Donaldson and Tilly watched anxiously.

Andy took a deep breath. Then he quickly cut the three bottom wires. The lights on the top of the fence went dead. The electricity was cut off!

Swiftly, the three men crawled under the fence. The German guards saw the lights go out. They shouted for the men to stop. But the men kept running. The Germans began firing their rifles. Donaldson felt bullets race past him. But still he didn't stop. He, Tilly, and Andy climbed through the last fence. Nothing could stop them now.

"We did it!" Donaldson cried. "We are free!"

And so they were. Donaldson, Tilly, and Andy had spent 28 days on the run. But they were free at last.

Do You Remember?

■ Read each sentence below. Write **T** if the sentence is true. Write **F** if the sentence is false.

_____ 1. Donaldson was a German soldier.

_____ 2. Mandel was too scared to try to escape.

_____ 3. Donaldson's first escape attempt failed.

_____ 4. Tilly and George were shot by Germans.

_____ 5. Mandel and George were captured and returned to prison.

_____ 6. Three fences separated Holland from Belgium.

_____ 7. Andy was killed while using the wirecutters.

_____ 8. German guards shot at Donaldson as he ran toward freedom.

Critical Thinking — Drawing Conclusions

■ Finish each sentence by writing the best answer.

1. Donaldson cut a hole in the roof of the cell because _____

   _____

2. Donaldson knew something had happened to George and Mandel

   because_____

   _____

3. The men needed to find a pair of wirecutters because _____

   _____

4. The Germans began firing at Donaldson, Andy, and Tilly because

   _____

Exploring Words

■ Use the clues to complete the puzzle. Choose from the words in the box.

lieutenant
combat
mission
line
discouraged
border
volts
spot
compass
barbed

Across
2. units of electricity
5. losing hope
7. fighting
9. a special job to be done

Down
1. what separates two countries
3. title of some army officers
4. having sharp points
6. see
7. a tool used to find directions
8. a group of soldiers side by side

Marching Out of Burma

"**B**y the time we get out of here, many of you will hate me. But I'll tell you one thing. You'll all get out."

General Joseph Stilwell **paused** and looked at the group of 114 men and women under his command. Among them were American Army officers, Burmese nurses, Chinese guards, and cooks. They were in Burma in the middle of World War II. The Japanese Army was closing in fast on the group. If Stilwell didn't get his people to India soon, they would be caught by the Japanese.

A Hard Way Out

Thousands of people were trying to escape to India. They filled the roads and made easy targets for the Japanese. Stilwell decided to take his people a different way. They would follow the road to Indaw. Then they would travel west on a little known path through the jungle.

On May 6, 1942, Stilwell and his group began their journey. It was a 140-mile trip. They would have to walk all the way. They would have to cross rivers and climb a 7,000-foot mountain range. The weather was hot and steamy. They would have to walk at least 14 miles a day.

The group had only one thing in its favor. And that was Joseph Stilwell. At age 59, he was a skilled leader with a strong **will.** When he set his mind on something, he almost always succeeded. Stilwell was a three-star general. But he dressed and lived like the soldiers under his command. "Uncle Joe" was known as being tough but fair.

The Long March

Stilwell prepared carefully for the march. He knew supplies were low, so he **rationed** the food. Each person would get only a small amount each day.

At the end of the first day, Stilwell sent his last radio messages. One of the messages was sent to an American officer in India. Stilwell told him of the route the party was taking. He asked the officer to send food and medicine to the town of Homalin near the Indian border. Then the radio was destroyed. It weighed almost 200 pounds – too much to carry.

Early in the morning, Stilwell led his people into the mountains. They suffered from the heat. It was the hottest time of the year in Burma. The temperature reached 100° F.

Stilwell knew it was important to move quickly. The Japanese couldn't be far behind. The group had little food. And the heavy rains could come at any time. The general tried to keep the group going. He kept up a fast walk of 105 steps per minute. He never slowed down – even when crossing rivers.

Soon, however, many became sick. Stilwell knew he had to slow down a bit. He gave the marchers 10 minutes rest every hour. The sickest people were carried by healthier ones. Many people suffered from **sunstroke**. Thorns, blisters, and leg sores also slowed down the marchers.

At one point, Colonel Williams, a doctor, was ready to quit. "We've got to stop. The sick just can't take any more," he begged.

Stilwell exploded. "This **column** can't stop. You and I can stand it. We're both older than any of them. Why can't they take it?"

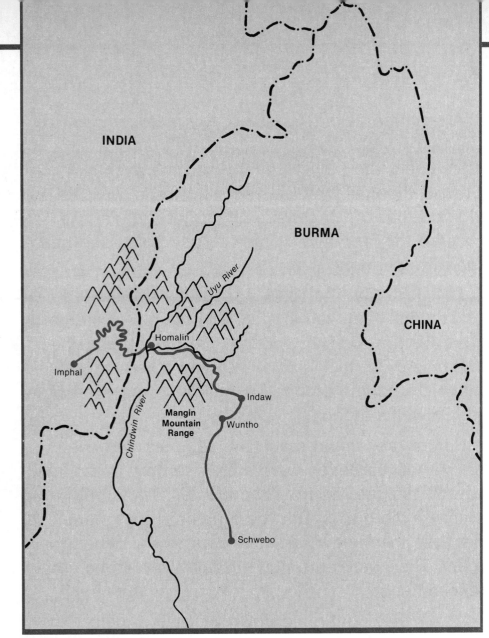

INDIA

BURMA

CHINA

Uyu River

Homalin

Imphal

Chindwin River

Indaw

Mangin Mountain Range

Wuntho

Schwebo

Map shows Stilwell's route out of Burma.

Stilwell **blasted** members of the group for being weak. His voice shook with anger. Still, the column moved very slowly. Stilwell had to cut the food rations in half to make them last longer. He ordered the marchers to take turns guarding the camp at night. During the day, he ordered scouts to go before the group to guard against Japanese attack. Everyone complained, but Stilwell didn't back down. He felt he had to be tough. People's lives depended on it.

On to India

After three days of walking, the marchers got to the Uyu River. There they found **rafts** and poles. They spent the night sailing down the river. But Stilwell thought they were moving too slowly. He worried that the Japanese might catch them. He ordered the men and women to use poles and push the rafts all night.

The next day, they saw a plane fly overhead. It circled and then came back. The people in the group were frightened. They thought the plane might be Japanese. But luck was with them. It was a British plane. The plane dropped supplies on the riverbanks for Stilwell's group.

Before they could reach the supplies, however, several of the boxes were stolen. People from nearby villages ran from the jungles. They took some of the boxes. But the marchers were happy because they knew someone was trying to help them. They were sure now that they would be **rescued** soon.

Again they continued down the river. Again they used poles to push the rafts all night. Then they walked across land to reach the town of Homalin. They hoped they would be rescued there or at least find the supplies they needed. But when they arrived, there was no food, no medicine, and not even a message.

All the marchers were disappointed. Some were angry. However, they had no choice but to go on. At last, on May 14, they got the help they had expected at Homalin. A British officer met the marchers. He had live pigs for them. He also said that more supplies were on the way. The marchers still faced

General Joseph Stilwell

five more days of walking. But now they had food and the promise of help ahead.

This same day, they began climbing up the mountains. Stilwell pushed them to walk 15 then 16 miles a day. The hard rains began. The trails became **slippery.** The marchers fell.

But on May 20, Stilwell and his party crossed the border into India. He had kept his promise. Every single person in the group made it. Many were sick. All of them were tired and hungry. Many had lost 20 or 30 pounds. But they were alive. All the other groups trying to escape from Burma had lost one or more people.

The 114 men and women knew they had Stilwell to thank. Some of them didn't like the way he had **treated** them. But they knew he had saved their lives. He had led by setting an example. He had suffered as much as they had. He had walked every mile they had walked. He ate only after everyone else had been fed. Without him to push them, many people would have simply given up. Uncle Joe Stilwell made sure that didn't happen.

Do You Remember?

■ Read each sentence below. Write **T** if the sentence is true. Write **F** if the sentence is false.

_____ 1. Stilwell led his group out of Japan.

_____ 2. Many died during the march.

_____ 3. Food supplies were limited.

_____ 4. The temperature in Burma sometimes reaches 100° F.

_____ 5. There are no jungles in Burma.

_____ 6. Stilwell carried the radio during the march.

_____ 7. The town of Homalin was near the Indian border.

_____ 8. Many people suffered from sunstroke.

Express Yourself

■ Pretend that you are Joe Stilwell. You are in the middle of the jungle with the group. Write a letter to your wife, Win Stilwell. Tell her what is happening and how you feel about it.

Dear Win,

_____

_____

_____

_____

_____

_____

Exploring Words

■ Use the words in the box to complete the paragraphs. Reread the paragraphs to be sure they make sense.

paused	sunstroke	rafts	slippery	column
rationed	blasted	will	treated	rescued

General Stilwell **(1)** _____ as he spoke to the group

under his command. Among them were American officers, Burmese

nurses, Chinese guards, and cooks. Then Joe Stilwell led the

(2) _____ of 114 people out of Burma. It was a difficult

march. Many people suffered from **(3)** _____. Others

caught diseases. Heavy rains came and made the path

(4) _____.

Often the marchers did not think they had the **(5)** _____

to keep going. Stilwell **(6)** _____ the group for being

weak. He **(7)** _____ them roughly to keep them moving.

He **(8)** _____ the food so that it would last. He found

(9) _____ to get them across the Uyu River. His skillful

leadership **(10)** _____ the group from the Japanese

Army.

Alone on a Raft

It was World War II. The German **submarine** waited for just the right target. On the morning of November 23, 1942, it sighted a British **merchant** ship, the Ben Lomond. The submarine fired a **torpedo** at the British ship.

The Ben Lomond sank quickly. Fifty-four of the 55 people on board died. Only one person **survived.** He was a 25-year-old **steward** named Poon Lim. Although he had lived through the blast, Poon Lim was in serious trouble. He was alone, swimming helplessly in the middle of the Atlantic Ocean.

The Raft

Luckily, one of the ship's rafts floated by. Poon Lim grabbed it and climbed on. He looked around for his **shipmates.** He didn't see anyone. All he saw was water.

Poon Lim's raft measured only six feet long by six feet wide. It had two containers on board. One held fresh water. The other contained chocolate, sugar, **biscuits,** fish paste, and a bottle of lime juice. There were also some flares that could be used to signal nearby ships. It wasn't much, but it was better than nothing.

Staying Alive

Poon Lim looked carefully at the food he had. He divided it up. He decided to eat only six biscuits a day. But he knew they wouldn't last very long.

Somehow he had to get more food. But how could he fish without a line or hook or bait?

As a child, Poon Lim had spent much time fishing. It was a good thing, for now he needed all his fishing skills. He had a piece of rope. But it was much too thick to use as a fishing line. So Poon Lim pulled out some of the threads. Then he took a pin that held one of the flares together and made a fish hook.

Finding bait was harder. Poon Lim made a paste from biscuit powder. But it just washed off the hook. Then he found some **barnacles** under the raft. He picked the meat out of the tough shells. The meat made pretty good bait. Poon Lim dropped his line over the side of the raft. After a while, he caught a fish.

"Little fish," he cried, "you have saved my life!"

Weeks and Weeks at Sea

Next Poon Lim caught a baby **shark.** He used its blood to **attract** other fish. Before long, he was able to scoop several small fish onto the raft. He didn't want to eat them all at once. He needed to make them last. So he tied rope to four posts on the raft. Then he hung the fish up so that they would dry.

After seven days on the raft, Poon Lim saw something in the distance. "It's a ship," he shouted. "I'm saved!"

Poon Lim fired his flares. But no one on the ship saw the tiny raft. The ship just sailed on. "It was my darkest day," Poon Lim said later.

But he didn't give up. He continued to fish. He found a way to collect fresh water. He sang songs to cheer himself up.

After about 100 days on the raft, his luck turned bad. For some reason, the fish stopped biting. He couldn't catch anything. Over the next few days, he ate all the fish he had stored. Then he went five days without food. At last, some birds landed on the raft. Poon Lim waited until dark. Then, while the birds slept, he caught 13 of them and tied them up.

"Now, at least, I'll eat," he thought to himself.

Poon Lim continued to drift for many more days. Then he noticed something strange. The water had changed color. It was more brown than before. That could mean only one thing. He was near land!

On April 5, 1943, a fishing boat from Brazil rescued him. Poon Lim had drifted halfway across the Atlantic Ocean. He had survived 133 days at sea in an open raft – longer than any other person on record.

Do You Remember?

■ In the blank, write the letter of the best ending for each sentence.

_____ 1. As a child, Poon Lim did a lot of
   a. flying.   b. fishing.   c. fighting.

_____ 2. Poon Lim used barnacles to
   a. keep warm.   b. catch fish.   c. make biscuits.

_____ 3. To stay cheerful, Poon Lim
   a. sang songs.   b. made flags.   c. played games.

_____ 4. On his raft, Poon Lim found some
   a. guns.   b. flares.   c. books.

_____ 5. Poon Lim was rescued by a
   a. helicopter.   b. submarine.   c. fishing boat.

Critical Thinking—Finding the Sequence

■ Number the sentences to show the order in which things happened in the story. The first one is done for you.

_____ Poon Lim noticed that the water was changing color.

_____ Poon Lim caught 13 birds.

__1__ The Ben Lomond was hit by a torpedo.

_____ Poon Lim tried to get the attention of a ship he saw in the distance.

_____ Poon Lim climbed onto the raft.

Exploring Words

■ Choose the correct word from the box to complete each sentence.

submarine	torpedo	shark	merchant	steward
shipmates	survive	biscuits	barnacles	attract

1. A _____ is a ship that can travel underwater.

2. To _____ means to live through something

dangerous.

3. People who sail on a ship together are called _____.

4. _____ are small sea animals with hard shells.

5. A ship full of things to be bought or sold is a _____

ship.

6. A bomb that travels underwater is called a _____.

7. A person who takes care of passengers on a ship is a

_____.

8. To _____ something means to bring it near.

9. In Britain, _____ are crackers or cookies.

10. A _____ is a dangerous fish with tough skin and

rows of sharp teeth.

Tumbling Through the Sky!

The sky over Germany was black. It was March 24, 1944 – the middle of World War II. British **Sergeant** Nicholas Alkemade could see straight down from the glass bubble in the back of his **bomber**. German **searchlights** were **scanning** the sky, looking for British planes. Alkemade checked his machine gun. It was ready.

Suddenly, he heard loud, crashing sounds. The glass in Alkemade's bubble **shattered**. His plane had been hit!

A Direct Hit

Alkemade grabbed his machine gun. He could see a German fighter plane moving toward him. It was less than 50 yards away! The German gunner opened fire. Quickly, Alkemade returned fire.

A stream of bullets flew back and forth. The German plane broke away. It was badly hit. Black smoke and flames shot out from one of the engines. But Alkemade didn't have much time to watch. His own plane was going down.

The British pilot radioed, "I can't hold her for long. You'll have to jump. Bail out! Bail out!"

No Parachute

Alkemade's bubble was very small. He didn't have room to store his parachute in it. He was wearing his parachute harness, but the chute itself was stored near the middle of the plane. Alkemade opened the door of the bubble to get it. Flames and smoke knocked him back.

He opened the door again and reached for the parachute. But it was too late. The chute was on fire. What could he do now? The plane was on fire at 18,000 feet. He was trapped with no parachute!

He sat frozen in his bubble. He knew in his heart that there was no hope.

The Impossible

The fire continued to spread. At any second, the plane might blow up. So Alkemade did the only thing he could. He jumped out of the plane without a parachute. He tumbled through the sky. It felt good to be away from the smoke and heat. He didn't feel like he was falling. He felt more like he was resting on a cloud.

As he fell, he gathered speed. Within seconds, he was traveling at a speed of 122 miles per hour. He was falling toward a patch of **fir** trees. But before he hit the trees, he fainted.

A few hours later, Alkemade opened his eyes. He looked up at the sky and blinked. He was alive! Above him he saw tall, snowy fir trees. All around him was soft, white snow. He had crashed through the branches of the trees and landed in a deep snowdrift. The branches had slowed his fall. The snow had **cushioned** his landing. He was alive!

An Unbelievable Story

Alkemade tried to sit up, but he couldn't. His back was hurt. He had burns on his face and legs. And his knee was **sprained.** A few hours later, he was found by German soldiers and taken to a hospital. During his hospital stay, he was questioned several times by German officers. They thought he was a

spy. They thought he had jumped from a plane and had hidden his parachute. When he told them what had happened, they became angry. They did not believe his story.

Three weeks later, Alkemade was moved to a prison. Here the commanding officer and other officers questioned him again. Alkemade repeated his story. He told the officers he could prove that he was telling the truth. Alkemade told them when and where his plane had fallen. He told them that they should go and look. They would find the burned remains of his parachute inside the plane. The Germans did as Alkemade instructed. They found his burned parachute in the middle of the plane. They knew that his **incredible** story must be true.

The officers shook his hand. The commanding officer said, "**Congratulations,** my boy, on being alive! What a story to tell your grandchildren!"

Do You Remember?

■ In the blank, write the letter of the best ending for each sentence.

_____ 1. Nicholas Alkemade was riding in the back of a
    a. British bomber.   b. German jet.   c. helicopter.

_____ 2. Alkemade didn't have his parachute because his bubble
    a. shattered.   b. was on fire.   c. was too small.

_____ 3. The pilot told Alkemade to
    a. check a map.   b. hold his fire.   c. bail out.

_____ 4. Alkemade's parachute
    a. burned.   b. ripped.   c. fell out of the plane.

_____ 5. Alkemade landed in
    a. water.   b. tall grass.   c. snow.

Express Yourself

■ Pretend you are Nicholas Alkemade. It is after the war. And you have been asked to speak in front of an audience. Tell the audience what the worst part of your adventure was.

_____

_____

_____

_____

_____

_____

_____

_____

Exploring Words

■ Use the clues to complete the puzzle. Choose from the words in the box.

sergeant
bomber
searchlights
scanned
shattered
fir
cushioned
sprain
incredible
congratulations

Across

3. what you say to show happiness for someone's good luck
5. to hurt a muscle by twisting it
8. an airplane that drops bombs
9. an officer in the Army

Down

1. hard to believe
2. type of tree
3. softened
4. large lights that search the sky
6. broke into many pieces
7. looked carefully

Train Ride to Freedom

Jaroslav Konvalinka stared at the calendar on his wall. Today was Tuesday, September 11, 1951. This was the big day. On this day he would put his **daring** plan into action.

Konvalinka got ready to go to work. Before he left, he told his wife to send word to their children's teachers that they were sick. He told her to take them to the train station. She and the children were to get on the train **headed** for Asch, Czechoslovakia.

Konvalinka's wife was alarmed. She didn't know what was going on.

A Bold Plan

Jaroslav Konvalinka worked as a train engineer in Czechoslovakia. But he was not happy living there. The Russians controlled the country. The people had very little freedom. Konvalinka **longed** to move his family to another country. But the Russians would not let them leave. They had put **roadblocks,** barbed wire fences, and guards all along the border between Czechoslovakia and West Germany.

Every day Konvalinka passed a set of old train tracks. They led out of Asch, Czechoslovakia, to Selb, West Germany. No one was allowed to use these tracks. The Russians had twisted the metal tracks to keep any train from trying to use them.

Konvalinka's plan was a bold one. He would do his job as an engineer. He would drive a train to Asch. When he got to Asch, however, he would not stop. He would try to drive the train over the twisted track to West Germany. He hoped that if the train was going fast enough, it would straighten the track and the train would not **derail.**

Heading for Asch

Konvalinka climbed into the engine of the train. He tried to stay **calm.** He didn't want the other workers to get **suspicious.** But as the morning passed, he grew nervous. At last, he reached a town called Franzenbad. It was the last stop before Asch. In Franzenbad, a friend named Karel Truksa got on board the train.

"Did you tell your wife what to do?" Konvalinka whispered to him.

Truksa nodded. "Yes. I told her to get on this train. But I didn't tell her why."

"I didn't tell my wife why either," Konvalinka said.

Both men knew it was safer that way. After all, the plan might not work. The train might derail. If that happened, Konvalinka and Truksa would probably be sentenced to death. But if their families didn't know anything about the plan, they might be allowed to live.

No Turning Back

When the train left Franzenbad, Truksa pulled out a gun. He ordered the fire tender to lie down on the floor. As he did this, Konvalinka said a silent prayer. He prayed that his wife and children had made it onto the train. But if they hadn't, he would never see them again. It was too late to turn back. He was going to make it to freedom on this day or be killed trying.

Konvalinka grabbed the **throttle** and pulled back on it. The train picked up speed. Soon it was going 65 miles per hour. It blew past the Asch station and headed for the twisted metal track. Konvalinka held his breath.

The train hit the twisted track with a sharp **jolt.** But it did not derail! The weight and speed of the train bent the track back into shape. The train raced toward the border. Russian guards ran out to set up a roadblock. But they were too late. They didn't even have time to fire their guns. Within minutes, the train reached West Germany.

Konvalinka hugged Truksa. "I feel a stone has fallen from my heart!" he cried. His joy grew when he saw that his wife and children were indeed on the train. The **entire** family was there. They were safe. Best of all, they were finally free.

Do You Remember?

■ In the blank, write the letter of the best ending for each sentence.

_____ 1. Konvalinka was
   a. a German spy.   b. an engineer.   c. a teacher.

_____ 2. Konvalinka told his wife to go to the
   a. school.   b. church.   c. train station.

_____ 3. Truksa and Konvalinka wanted to escape to
   a. Russia.   b. Poland.   c. West Germany.

_____ 4. Russians guarded the
   a. trains.   b. border.   c. schools.

_____ 5. The track between Asch and Selb was
   a. brand new.   b. rusty.   c. twisted.

Critical Thinking — Fact or Opinion?

■ A **fact** can be proven. An **opinion** is a belief. Opinions cannot be proven.

Write **F** before each statement that is a fact. Write **O** before each statement that is an opinion.

_____ 1. Konvalinka was wrong not to tell his wife about the plan.

_____ 2. Truksa brought a gun on board the train.

_____ 3. Konvalinka and Truksa tried to protect their families.

_____ 4. The Russians should have allowed people to cross the border freely.

_____ 5. In 1951, Russia controlled Czechoslovakia.

_____ 6. It was wrong for Konvalinka and Truksa to put people's lives in danger.

_____ 7. The train reached the speed of 65 miles per hour.

_____ 8. Konvalinka was the luckiest man in the world.

Exploring Words

■ Read each sentence. Fill in the circle next to the best meaning for the word in dark print. If you need help, use the Glossary.

1. The word **daring** means
   ○ a. tall.   ○ b. very unhappy.   ○ c. willing to take chances.

2. The word **headed** means
   ○ a. felt sad.   ○ b. asked.   ○ c. going in a certain direction.

3. The word **longed** means
   ○ a. drove.   ○ b. wanted.   ○ c. carried.

4. The word **roadblock** means
   ○ a. painted line.
   ○ b. something put across a road.
   ○ c. door.

5. The word **derail** means
   ○ a. run off the track.   ○ b. sign.   ○ c. mix up.

6. The word **calm** means
   ○ a. walk into.   ○ b. windy.   ○ c. not excited.

7. The word **suspicious** means
   ○ a. feeling that something is wrong.
   ○ b. rich.
   ○ c. full of spices.

8. The word **throttle** means
   ○ a. drink.
   ○ b. lever that controls speed.
   ○ c. different colors.

9. The word **jolt** means
   ○ a. put together.   ○ b. lock.   ○ c. jerk.

10. The word **entire** means
    ○ a. clothing.   ○ b. whole.   ○ c. plain.

Crash Landing!

S pence Black dropped a coin into the pay phone. He called his home in Dallas, Texas. The maid answered.

Spence said, "I'm calling to let you know Beth and I are running late. Tell the children that everything is all right. We should be home in an hour."

Spence hung up. Then he and his wife Beth walked onto the Fort Worth airfield. They climbed into their small private airplane and took off. It was 9:00 P.M. on May 14, 1960.

Trouble in the Sky

The night was calm and clear. It was a perfect night for flying. Beth leaned back in her seat to enjoy the ride. Spence was an **experienced** pilot and was at the **controls.**

"I love flying at night. Don't you?" Spence asked.

Beth nodded. But then, all at once, something happened. Spence let go of the controls and grabbed his **chest.** He tried to speak but couldn't. Instead, he **slumped** forward in his seat. Beth screamed out Spence's name, but he didn't answer. He was having a heart attack.

Panic washed over Beth. She screamed Spence's name again. But still he did not answer. Beth could see he was in trouble. His eyes were cloudy, and he was having a hard time breathing.

Beth reached across her husband's body and grabbed the wheel with one hand. She knew what to do to make the airplane go left, right, up, or down. She managed to steady the plane and keep it from crashing. Beth didn't know that she could have changed the controls over to her side.

With her free hand, she picked up the radio **microphone.** Beth remembered seeing Spence push a button when he spoke into it. She pushed the button and screamed into the microphone.

"Help me! Won't somebody please help me!"

A Close Call

No one answered her. Beth hung up the microphone. When she looked back at Spence, she could tell he was dying. Tears ran down Beth's face. She didn't think she could go on without him. She wanted to die, too. She turned the plane around to head away from Dallas. She thought she could crash the plane in an open field. This way, no one else would be hurt.

But then she thought of her five children. If she and Spence both died, who would take care of them? How could she leave them without a father or a mother?

Beth knew what she had to do. She had to be there for her children. That meant she had to land the plane safely. She wiped her eyes and took a deep breath. She began looking for the lights of Dallas Love Field Airport. She also began sending new radio messages.

"SOS, Love Field! I'm in trouble, terrible trouble. Please help me!"

Beth didn't know if anyone could hear her. But a controller at Love Field, Donald Potter, heard her call for help. He tried to reach her by radio. But Beth kept switching **channels**, so he couldn't reach her. Potter thought she would soon try to land. He ordered all other planes off the **runways.** He told firefighters and crash trucks to stand by. And he watched for some sign of her approach.

As Beth Black reached Love Field, she saw a string of lights. She thought it was the runway, and so she pointed the plane toward it. But it wasn't the runway. She had gone past the airport. She was heading right for a highway! The lights she had seen were the lights along the highway.

Donald Potter saw what was happening. "Pull up, pull up!" he cried into his radio.

At last, he found Beth's channel. She heard his warning. At the same time she saw the traffic on the highway. She pulled back on the wheel just in time. The plane rose higher into the air.

Potter had to get her back to Love Field. "Turn around! Turn around!" he told her.

Beth swung the plane around. She flew back toward the airport. This time she spotted the runway lights. When she saw runway 31, she pushed the steering wheel forward. Again the plane dropped lower in the sky.

Crash Landing

As the plane came down, it was shaking madly. Beth could see that the plane was moving too fast for a safe landing. She could also tell that she was coming in at too steep an **angle.** But she didn't know how to slow down. And she didn't know how to adjust the angle of the plane. She heard Donald Potter talking to her over the radio. But she couldn't understand what he was telling her.

As she approached the runway, Beth prayed. "Please let me live for the sake of the children."

Then, a few seconds before landing, she remembered something. Spence always pushed a couple of buttons before landing. Quickly, she searched the instruments. She found a button marked "flaps." She pushed it, and instantly the plane slowed down. Then she pushed a second button marked "landing **gear.**"

The plane was still going too fast to land. Beth didn't know what to do. In a last **desperate** move, she reached over her husband's body. She turned the key and shut off the engine. Then, stretched out across Spence, she fainted.

Donald Potter and others watched in fear as the plane hit the runway. It bounced 40 feet into the air. Then it landed again about 300 yards away. The engine snapped off in the crash. The wings and body were crushed. It didn't look like anyone could have lived through the crash.

But rescue workers found Beth Black sitting on one of the crushed airplane wings. Her left arm was broken, and her jaw was cracked. But she was alive.

"Please help my husband," she said. Then she added, "Would somebody please go and tell the children we're home?"

Rescue workers found that Spence Black had died before the plane ever landed. The heart attack had killed him.

Later, Beth Black talked about her escape from death. "By rights, I should have been killed in the crash at Love Field, but I wasn't. Now it's my job to make the most of this wonderful gift of life."

Do You Remember?

■ Read each sentence below. Write **T** if the sentence is true. Write **F** if the sentence is false.

_____ 1. Spence Black did not know how to fly an airplane.

_____ 2. Beth Black had never landed an airplane.

_____ 3. Spence died of a heart attack.

_____ 4. Donald Potter thought Beth was joking when he got her radio message.

_____ 5. Beth landed the plane in Salt Lake City, Utah.

_____ 6. Beth turned off the engine before the plane hit the ground.

_____ 7. The plane was badly damaged during the landing.

_____ 8. Beth walked away from the crash without any injuries.

Express Yourself

■ Pretend you are a newspaper reporter. Write a story telling about Beth Black's experience. Tell who, what, when, where, and why.

_____

_____

_____

_____

_____

_____

_____

Exploring Words

■ Use the words in the box to complete the paragraphs. Reread the paragraphs to be sure they make sense.

runway	angle	experienced	microphone	chest
slumped	gear	desperate	channels	controls

Spence Black was an **(1)** _____ pilot. But on May 14, 1960, he had a heart attack in his plane. He grabbed his

(2) _____ and **(3)** _____ forward in his seat.

His wife, Beth, picked up the radio **(4)** _____ and

asked for help. She changed **(5)** _____ many times,

hoping to get an answer. As each second passed, she felt more

and more **(6)** _____.

At last, she heard Donald Potter's voice. He helped her find

the airport and the **(7)** _____. She figured out how

to use some of the plane's **(8)** _____. She lowered the

landing **(9)** _____. The plane came down at a very

sharp **(10)** _____. Beth was hurt, but she lived

through the crash.

Prison Break!

Prisoner Frank Morris stared at the gray stone building. "So this is The Rock," he muttered to himself.

The Rock was Alcatraz, a prison in San Francisco **Bay**. America's toughest prisoners were sent here. No one had ever escaped from this prison. Prison **officials** believed no one ever would.

But Morris felt differently. The iron bars on the windows didn't scare him. The 15-foot fences didn't either. Morris didn't want to be here. And he didn't plan to stay.

Alcatraz Prison

An Impossible Idea

Alcatraz opened in 1934. When Morris arrived about 25 years later, there had been 11 escape **attempts.** All had failed.

Morris soon learned why escape was impossible. For its size, Alcatraz had more guards per prisoner than any other prison. Few visitors were allowed. Guards searched all visitors carefully. Prisoners were allowed to do very little. And they were always watched. They were locked in their cells 14 hours a day from 5:30 P.M. to 7:30 A.M. Guards checked on them every hour while they were in their cells.

Even if a prisoner did break out, there was no place to go. Alcatraz was built on a small, rocky island. The **mainland** was nearly two miles away. The bay water was freezing. And its swift **currents** would sweep away almost any swimmer.

Still, Frank Morris wanted to escape. Morris felt that no prison could hold him. He had been arrested for armed robbery, and he had already broken out of one prison in Louisiana. He planned to break out of here, too.

Morris got two prisoners to join him. They were John and Clarence Anglin. Like Morris, these brothers were armed robbers with long prison sentences. They believed in Morris. They felt he could lead them to freedom.

The Escape Plan

"We must be very careful," Morris warned them. "And we must take our time. An escape from Alcatraz cannot be rushed. But if all goes well, we can escape.

"First, we'll need to steal some spoons from the dining hall," Morris said. "We'll sharpen them and use them to dig through the cell wall. Each cell has a **vent.** I checked the **concrete** around my vent. It's pretty weak. We should each be able to dig a hole big enough to slip through."

"But the guards will catch us digging the holes!" cried Clarence.

"Not if we're quiet. We'll work at night between bed checks. During the day, we'll cover the holes with cardboard. We can paint the cardboard so it looks like the vent. Also, we'll need some hair from the **barbershop**. We'll use it to make **fake** heads. Those will stay on our pillows the night we escape. That should fool the guards during the bed checks. They won't know we're missing until morning. By then, we'll be long gone."

As Morris talked, the Anglin brothers grew more

and more excited. This plan might work. They might really break out of The Rock.

The men worked very hard for many months digging through the concrete walls. Each day they carried the concrete they had chipped off and scattered it around the prison yard. The three also spent much time carefully making and painting the fake heads.

Prison officials never figured out how the three men were able to get all the supplies they needed. Nor could officials understand how the men were able to hide their work for so long. Each cell was searched often by guards.

Over the Wall

Morris put his escape plan into action on the night of June 11, 1962. Just after the 9:30 P.M. bed check, he signaled to the Anglin brothers. It was time to make their move. Quietly, they stuffed their beds with pillows. They put the fake heads in place. Then they carefully removed the cardboard vents. They squeezed through the holes they had made in the cell walls. Then they put back the cardboard vents. To the passing guards, everything in the prisoners' cells looked fine. No one knew about the escape until 7:15 the next morning.

Meanwhile, the three prisoners had plenty to do. They had escaped from their cells. But they still had to get out of the prison. The vents led to a tunnel. At the end of the tunnel, they found pipes leading to the roof. They climbed them. Somehow, they managed to bend a steel bar that blocked their way.

On the roof they were in full view of the gun tower. Morris and the two brothers dashed 100 feet across the roof. No one saw them. Then they slid down a 40-foot pipe to the ground. Lights swept across the prison yard. Still, no one saw them. The three men climbed a 15-foot fence and dropped to the ground.

They were out of the prison. But they were still on the island. They ran down to the shore. No one really knows what the men did next.

| Frank Morris | John Anglin | Clarence Anglin |

Prison officials later learned that the three **criminals** had planned to use a raft made from raincoats to get to the mainland. Once there, they planned to rob a clothing store.

The next morning, police searched everywhere for the three prisoners. They found a paddle floating about 200 yards from Angel Island. Angel Island is two miles from Alcatraz. They thought they would find the bodies, too. After all, the men didn't have much of a raft. Police did not think they could possibly have made it across the rough stretch of water to the mainland.

But the bodies were never found. To this day, no one knows what happened to Frank Morris and the Anglin brothers. They were never seen again. The three may have drowned in San Francisco Bay. Or they may have been the only men ever to escape from The Rock.

Do You Remember?

■ In the blank, write the letter of the best ending for each sentence.

_____ 1. The men dug through the walls with
   a. their hands.   b. shovels.   c. spoons.

_____ 2. Morris and the Anglin brothers made a raft out of
   a. shoe leather.   b. raincoats.   c. pillows.

_____ 3. The guards did not discover the escape until
   a. morning.   b. a week later.   c. Christmas.

_____ 4. Morris and the Anglin brothers made fake heads to
   a. keep warm.   b. pass time.   c. fool the guards.

_____ 5. Police never found the
   a. fake heads.   b. paddle.   c. men.

Critical Thinking — Main Ideas

■ Underline the two most important ideas from the story.

1. Frank Morris planned a daring escape from Alcatraz prison.

2. Frank Morris and the Anglin brothers were armed robbers.

3. Prisoners were locked in their cells 14 hours a day.

4. Alcatraz is two miles from the mainland.

5. Frank Morris and the Anglin brothers disappeared after breaking

   out of The Rock.

Exploring Words

■ Use the clues to complete the puzzle. Choose from the words in the box.

| bay |
| officials |
| attempts |
| mainland |
| currents |
| criminal |
| vent |
| concrete |
| barbershop |
| fake |

Across

2. place where hair is cut
6. not real
7. an opening through which air passes
9. the main part of a continent
10. flowing water

Down

1. person who breaks the law
3. tries
4. water that is partly surrounded by land
5. people in charge
8. what the prison walls were made of

Hijacking!

Captain William Haas asked for a cup of coffee. Flight **attendant** Donna Holman went back to the **galley** to get it. Suddenly she felt a hand across her mouth. She saw a gun and froze in fear. A **terrorist** named Henry Jackson held her tightly. Jackson waved the gun. He wanted all of the 27 passengers aboard Southern Flight 49 to see it.

"Nobody move!" he shouted. "We're taking over! And let's not have any heroes because they'll be dead heroes."

This Is a Hijacking!

Louis Moore and Melvin Cale jumped up from their seats. They, too, were terrorists. And they also had guns. The passengers sat quietly. No one knew what to do. Everyone was afraid of what might happen next.

Donna Holman looked at her watch. It was 6:00 P.M. on November 10, 1972. This flight had just taken off from Birmingham, Alabama. It was supposed to fly to the nearby city of Montgomery, Alabama. It should have been a 20-minute flight. But clearly, things had changed.

While still holding Donna Holman, Jackson burst into the **cockpit.** He shoved the gun in Captain Haas' face. Holman's voice cracked with fear as she cried, "This is a **hijacking.** He's not kidding."

Haas stayed calm. He knew that was the only way he could save the lives of his passengers. He said, "Keep calm. We don't want anyone hurt. We'll obey your instructions."

Hijacking!

Jackson shouted his demands. "Get this plane to Detroit! We want $10 million from the city of Detroit. If we don't get it, we're going to start killing people on this plane."

Getting Even

The mayor of Detroit couldn't believe his ears. "Are you kidding? That much money? Why would they want it from the city?"

Jackson and Moore wanted to get even with the city. They said the police there had beaten them after they had been arrested. The two men had **sued** the city for $4 million. When the city offered them just $25 to settle the case, they were furious. They got some guns and decided to hijack a plane and demand the money. Cale, Moore's half brother, had gone along with them.

The mayor of Detroit stalled. Meanwhile, Southern Flight 49 kept circling the airport. After a while, the plane ran low on gas. Jackson told Haas to get more gas at the Cleveland airport. After this was

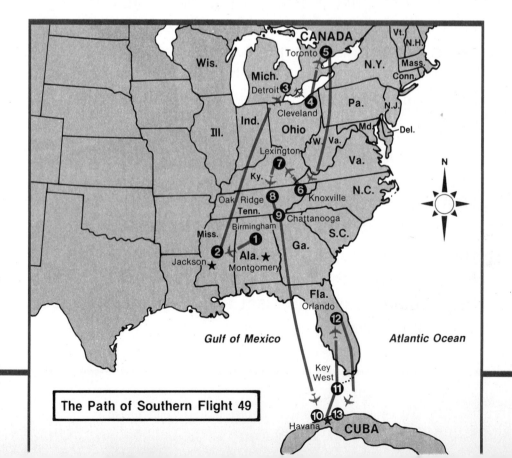

The Path of Southern Flight 49

done, he told Haas to fly to Toronto, Canada. There the hijackers were offered $500,000. But they angrily turned it down.

Jackson screamed, "We're tired of all this. We're taking this plane to Oak Ridge, Tennessee. We'll dive it into a **nuclear reactor**."

By this time, it was early in the morning of November 11. Haas **wearily** pointed the plane toward Tennessee. When they got there, Jackson pressed his gun against Haas' head.

"Dive it into a reactor," he commanded.

Haas had to think fast. The sky was cloudy. Maybe he could fool Jackson. Haas said, "I can't. There's no way to tell where the reactors are."

Jackson gave in. He agreed to wait one more hour. But he repeated his demands. If he didn't get the money, he would crash the plane.

Just before 1:00 P.M., Southern Airline officials radioed the hijackers that their money was at the Chatanooga, Tennessee, airport. Jackson let Haas land the plane at the airport. There police gave him $2 million. The police knew it wasn't $10 million. But they also knew that the hijackers wouldn't have time to count it. Then Jackson ordered Haas to fly to Havana, Cuba. He demanded to see Fidel Castro, the leader of Cuba.

Escape From Terror

The Cubans wanted nothing to do with the hijackers. When the plane arrived, Castro refused to see Jackson. After the plane had been on the ground for an hour, the Cubans partly filled its tanks with gasoline. Jackson ordered Haas to take it up quickly. The plane then flew to Key West, Florida, for more gasoline.

By this time, the hijackers had controlled the plane for 22 hours. Jackson no longer seemed sure what he wanted. He told Haas to fly to Switzerland. Haas told him the plane couldn't fly across the Atlantic. Jackson then ordered him to fly to Orlando, Florida.

Police in Orlando decided to shoot out the plane's tires after it landed. That way the plane couldn't take off again. Once the tires were shot out, police planned to rush into the plane and rescue the passengers and crew.

But police were only able to shoot out the tires on the left side of the plane. When the hijackers heard the noise, they began firing at the police. Jackson turned to the copilot. "You did it! You told them to do it! We're going to kill you!"

Jackson shot the copilot in the arm. He tried to shoot him again, but his gun **jammed.** Luckily,

Moore stepped in. "That's enough. Don't kill him. We may need him. Let's get out of here."

"They've blown our tires. We can't go anyplace," Haas said.

Jackson yelled at Haas. "Get into the air, or we'll start killing people!"

Somehow Haas got the plane in the air. But he knew the plane could only land one more time. He told the hijackers this. Jackson told Haas to go back to Cuba. Haas radioed the Cubans to get ready for what could be a crash landing.

The flight attendants prepared the passengers for the landing. They explained what to do during and after the landing. Some of the passengers shook hands with each other and said good-by. Then they all waited.

Carefully, Haas brought the plane down onto the runway. Sparks flew as the left wheels hit the ground. Smoke poured out as the plane dragged to a halt. The hijackers jumped out the door. They ran across a nearby field. But the Cubans quickly arrested them.

And so, finally, Southern Flight 49 came to an end. The hijacking had lasted 30 hours and covered 4,000 miles.

Most of the time Captain Haas had flown the plane with a gun held to his head. But his calmness had helped to calm the hijackers. Throughout the hijacking, his only thoughts were of the safety of his passengers and crew.

When the passengers saw Captain Haas inside the airport, they gave him a big cheer. They knew he had saved their lives. Without his skill and **courage,** the hijackers might have killed them all.

Do You Remember?

■ Read each sentence below. Write **T** if the sentence is true. Write **F** if the sentence is false.

_____ 1. The hijackers shot Donna Holman in the arm.

_____ 2. The flight lasted 30 hours.

_____ 3. The terrorists demanded $10 million from the city of Detroit.

_____ 4. Fidel Castro refused to see the hijackers.

_____ 5. Haas agreed to fly the plane to Switzerland.

_____ 6. Police tried to shoot out the plane's tires.

_____ 7. Haas made a crash landing at Oak Ridge, Tennessee.

_____ 8. The copilot of the plane died.

Express Yourself

■ Imagine you are one of the passengers on Southern Flight 49. Write a letter home explaining why you will be arriving late.

_____

_____

_____

_____

_____

_____

_____

Exploring Words

■ Choose the correct word from the box to complete each sentence.

nuclear reactor	**sued**	**galley**	**attendant**	**courage**
terrorist	**jammed**	**cockpit**	**hijacking**	**wearily**

1. The place where the pilot of an airplane sits is the _____.

2. A person who helps passengers on an airplane is called a flight

   _____.

3. Taking control of an airplane and forcing it to go somewhere

   is called _____.

4. If you are tired, you move and talk _____.

5. Someone who uses violence to get what he or she wants is a

   _____.

6. The kitchen of an airplane is called a _____.

7. Someone who is very brave has a lot of _____.

8. A _____ is a part of a power plant that makes a

   large amount of energy and heat.

9. To be taken to court by someone who wants money from you

   is to be _____.

10. If something gets stuck or locked in position, it is

   _____.

Survival in Cambodia

Dith Pran sat under a tree in Dam Dek, Cambodia. Slowly, he ate a spoonful of rice. His stomach **rumbled** with hunger. But there was nothing more to eat. Each person was allowed only one spoonful of rice a day.

Pran's legs **cramped** and felt weak. His head ached. "I must get something more to eat," he thought.

That night he sneaked out to the rice fields. He reached down and grabbed a handful of rice.

Suddenly, a voice shouted, "Thief! Thief!"

Pran's heart froze. He had been seen.

A Dangerous Past

Dith Pran expected to be killed for his crime. Khmer Rouge (kuh MER roozh) leaders killed anyone who broke their rules. The Khmer Rouge had taken over Cambodia (also known as Kampuchea) in 1975. Since then, three million people had been killed, had starved, or had died of disease. The Khmer Rouge forced all **survivors** to work for them. Anyone who complained was killed.

Pran had tried to **blend** in with the other workers. He didn't want the Khmer Rouge to know that he was educated. The Khmer Rouge killed anyone who was a soldier, a teacher, or had an education. In the early 1970's, Pran had worked as a **translator** for an American newspaper. The Khmer Rouge hated the United States and all Western countries. If they found out about Pran's past, they would kill him immediately.

Cambodian soldiers

Pran stole the rice in October of 1975. He was tired of eating grasshoppers, snails, and rat meat to satisfy his hunger. He didn't want to get in trouble. But his hunger was **overwhelming.** He took a chance, and he was caught.

Keeping the Dream Alive

The Khmer Rouge did not kill Pran. They beat him until he was almost dead. Then they made him get up and go back to work.

Pran knew he was lucky to be alive. But he also knew he was being watched. He had to escape from Dam Dek and find a way to get out of Cambodia.

Pran dreamed of escaping to the **neighboring** country of Thailand (TY land). But Thailand was nearly 80 miles away. To get there, he would have to walk through jungles. He would have to get past dozens of Khmer Rouge soldiers. It seemed impossible. Still, Pran never let the dream die.

Dith Pran

In 1978, Pran was moved to a different village. This one was 20 miles closer to the Thailand border. Here Pran worked as hard as ever. But again he felt himself being watched. He still saw no chance of escaping. In January of 1979, Vietnamese soldiers took control of Cambodia. But they, too, hated the West. So Pran's life remained in danger.

Pran was allowed to return to his home village. Here he learned his father had starved to death. Three brothers and one sister had been killed by soldiers. Only Pran, his mother, and a sister had survived.

Through the Jungle

In September of 1979, Pran felt he could wait no longer. He had to get to Thailand. Late one night he

Refugee camp

crept out of the village. He ran into the jungles and followed streams. He stayed alive by eating bugs and tree bark. Every step he took brought new danger. Khmer Rouge soldiers still **roamed** this area freely. They set many **deadly** traps. They also left bombs hidden under leaves and vines.

Pran had many close calls. But after four days, he reached the border. He was afraid to go any farther. He feared guards might be watching him. For 17 days Pran hid near the border.

On October 3, Pran finally made his move. He ran across the border and into Thailand. For 15 miles he ran. At last he came to a **refugee** camp. There he was given food and shelter. He sent word to his American friends that he was alive. These friends quickly flew him to the United States. There, at last, Dith Pran found freedom.

Do You Remember?

■ Read each sentence below. Write **T** if the sentence is true. Write **F** if the sentence is false.

_____ 1. Dith Pran was caught stealing rice.

_____ 2. The Khmer Rouge hated all Western countries.

_____ 3. Dith Pran did not want to leave Cambodia.

_____ 4. Khmer Rouge soldiers set traps in the jungle.

_____ 5. Dith Pran always had plenty to eat.

_____ 6. Dith Pran refused to go to the United States.

_____ 7. Vietnamese soldiers shot Dith Pran.

_____ 8. Dith Pran escaped the Khmer Rouge by sneaking into Thailand.

Critical Thinking—Cause and Effect

■ Complete the following sentences.

1. Dith Pran tried to steal rice because _____

_____

2. Dith Pran kept his past job a secret because _____

_____

3. Dith Pran was badly beaten because _____

_____

4. Dith Pran hid near the Thailand border for 17 days because_____

_____

_____

Exploring Words

■ Read each sentence. Fill in the circle next to the best meaning for the word in dark print. If you need help, use the Glossary.

1. Dith Pran's stomach **rumbled** with hunger.
   o a. turned blue   o b. opened up   o c. made noise

2. His legs felt **cramped.**
   o a. long   o b. full of pain   o c. very powerful

3. The **survivors** worked in the fields.
   o a. people who remained alive   o b. doctors   o c. boys

4. Dith Pran tried to **blend** in with the others.
   o a. mix   o b. move backwards   o c. stand still

5. Dith Pran's hunger was **overwhelming.**
   o a. too strong to ignore   o b. easy to see   o c. gone

6. Dith Pran had worked as a **translator** for a newspaper.
   o a. reporter
   o b. artist
   o c. someone who changes one language into another

7. He went to the **neighboring** country of Thailand.
   o a. rich   o b. nearby   o c. full of dirt and disease

8. He **roamed** the jungle for days.
   o a. wandered   o b. stayed away from   o c. feared

9. The Khmer Rouge set **deadly** traps.
   o a. able to kill   o b. animal   o c. secret

10. Dith Pran made it to a **refugee** camp.
    o a. soldier
    o b. child
    o c. person who leaves home to escape danger

Balloon Ride to Freedom

"We've got to get out of here. We have to escape," said Peter Strelzyk.

"Yes, but how?" asked Gunter Wetzel. "We can't walk across the border. The guards will shoot us. And we can't swim across. There are bombs all along the banks of the river."

Peter whispered, "We could cross the border in a hot air balloon."

"And where do we find a hot air balloon?" laughed Gunter.

"We don't find one. We make our own," replied Peter.

Peter Strelzyk

Gunter Wetzel

Early Problems

Peter Strelzyk and Gunter Wetzel lived in East Germany. The two men didn't like living there. The **Communists** controlled East Germany. And the Communists didn't allow people much freedom.

The two men decided that to find freedom, they would have to cross the border. They would have to take their families to West Germany.

On March 7, 1978, Peter came up with the idea of the balloon. The two men knew nothing about balloons. And they couldn't find any books on the **subject.** But they decided to make a balloon anyway. They bought 880 yards of brown cotton in a nearby town. They told the salesperson they were making tents for young people at a camp.

They took the material to Gunter's house. Secretly, they worked on the balloon in the attic. Gunter and his wife, Petra, sewed the cotton into the shape of a balloon. Peter built a little **platform** for it.

After six weeks, the balloon was ready to test. The two men drove to a lonely field. They tried to **inflate** the balloon, but nothing happened. The air just leaked through the cotton. They had used the wrong kind of **material.**

Sadly, they took the balloon home. They cut it into small pieces and burned it.

Another Failure

For several months, Peter and Gunter looked for a better type of cloth to use. Finally, they decided on **taffeta.** Air wouldn't leak through taffeta. They drove to a different town to buy the 880 yards of material. This time they told the salesperson they belonged to a sailing club.

As the second balloon took shape, Gunter started to have second thoughts. Petra feared the escape wouldn't work. After discussing it with Peter, Gunter decided not to try to escape.

Peter Strelzyk continued to work on the balloon alone. In June 1979, the balloon was finished. Peter and his family waited for the right weather. On the night of July 3, the wind began blowing toward the West German border.

They packed up their two children and drove out of town. At a quiet spot near the border, Peter inflated the balloon. It took him just five minutes.

The four of them jumped onto the tiny platform. The balloon rose slowly into the sky. For 34 minutes, it stayed up. Then a thick fog moved into the area. The balloon became wet. The extra weight dragged it back to the ground. The balloon and the Strelzyks landed in the woods.

Peter looked around in panic. Were they in East

The balloon the two families made is shown spread
on the ground.

Germany or West Germany? He saw the high wire
fences that marked the border. With a sinking heart,
he knew he was on the wrong side of it. He and his
family were still in East Germany.

Quickly, he led his family back to the car. They
got home before the police saw them. But they had
to leave their balloon stuck in the treetops.

Success at Last!

Within a few days, the police found the wrecked
balloon. The news spread fast. Soon everyone knew
about the failed escape. Police looked everywhere
for **clues.** They **vowed** to find the owners of the
balloon and put them in jail.

Peter was afraid. He had to build a new balloon. And he had to build it fast. Later that month, he talked to Gunter.

"We can't do it without you," Peter said. "Please come with us."

Gunter talked to his family. A week later, he gave his answer. "We'll come."

This time, they had to be more careful. They didn't dare buy the 880 yards of cloth they needed from one store. That would make the police suspicious. So, each day they drove to different towns. They bought a few yards here and a few yards there. In all, they drove more than 2,400 miles and went to nearly 100 towns. The two families used all the money they had in savings.

Officers show gas tanks on the balloon.

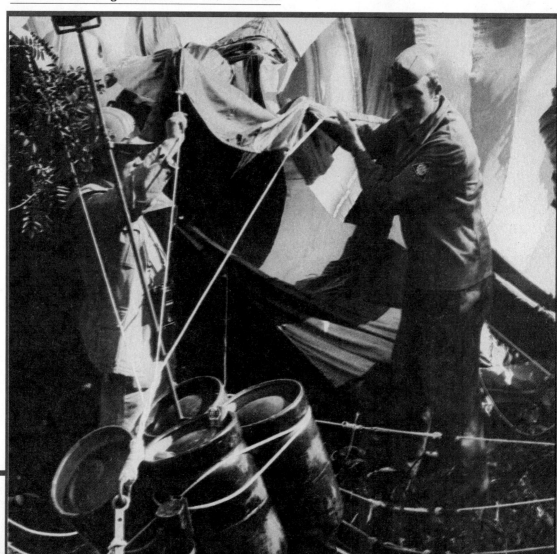

76

At last they had all the cloth they needed. For weeks they worked around-the-clock sewing the pieces together. Then, finally, they finished the third balloon. It was one of the largest hot air balloons ever made in Europe.

On September 15, they were ready to try again. Late that night, the two families drove out of town. On an empty field, they filled the balloon with hot air. Then all eight people hopped on board. The balloon rose into the night sky.

Soon they were 6,500 feet above the ground. Then suddenly, they saw searchlights. Had one of the border guards seen them? Would they be shot out of the sky?

Peter turned up the flame for the balloon. The balloon rose to 8,500 feet. The searchlight couldn't shine that high. But at this **height,** it was freezing cold. The children **huddled** together trying not to cry.

For 23 minutes, they stayed high in the air. But then they ran out of gas, and the flame went out. The balloon began to fall. Five minutes later, it hit the ground with a thud.

The two families did not know if they were safe. Leaving their wives and children hidden, the two men walked toward a barn.

A police car approached them. The two men swallowed hard as the police officers got out of their car.

"Are we in West Germany?" Peter asked.

"Yes," answered one of the police officers.

Peter and Gunter hugged each other in joy. "We've done it! We've done it!" they cried. And so they had. They were the first people ever to fly a balloon to freedom.

Do You Remember?

■ In the blank, write the letter of the best ending for each sentence.

_____ 1. Peter Strelzyk and Gunter Wetzel wanted to get to
   a. East Germany.　　b. West Germany.　　c. Poland.

_____ 2. The balloon made of cotton cloth
   a. burned up.　　b. leaked air.　　c. was too heavy.

_____ 3. Peter Strelzyk and his family left the second balloon in the
   a. treetops.　　b. ocean.　　c. back of a police car.

_____ 4. During the escape, the children became
   a. cold.　　b. sick.　　c. angry.

_____ 5. The third balloon carried
   a. Peter and his wife.
   b. Gunter.
   c. Peter, Gunter, and their families.

Express Yourself

■ Pretend you are the son or daughter of Peter Strelzyk. You and your family have escaped by balloon to West Germany. Write a letter to a friend in East Germany describing your escape.

Dear _____,

_____

_____

_____

_____

_____

_____

Exploring Words

■ Use the words in the box to complete the paragraphs. Reread the paragraphs to be sure they make sense.

Communists	subject	clues	material	taffeta
huddled	vowed	height	platform	inflate

Peter Strelzyk and Gunter Wetzel did not like living in East Germany because it was controlled by **(1)** _____. They wanted to take their families to West Germany. They discussed the **(2)** _____ of how to escape. Finally, they decided to escape in a hot air balloon.

Their first balloon was made of the wrong **(3)** _____. It leaked when they tried to **(4)** _____ it. They made a second balloon of **(5)** _____. This balloon floated, but it fell to the ground before reaching West Germany. It was later found by police who **(6)** _____ they would put the owners in jail.

The third balloon worked better. It took the Strelzyk and Wetzel families to a **(7)** _____ of 8,500 feet. The families **(8)** _____ together on the **(9)** _____ of the balloon as it floated west. When they landed, they searched for **(10)** _____ to find out where they were. They were happy when they learned they had made it to West Germany.

Lawyer Turns Outlaw

Lawyer Mary Evans

T im Kirk sat in a small room in Brushy Mountain State Prison in Knoxville, Tennessee. Across from him sat his **lawyer**, Mary Evans. She would be defending the 36-year-old prisoner against the new **charges** brought against him.

Kirk's **trial** was to start soon. He was already serving a 65-year sentence for **armed robbery.** Now he was accused of killing two prisoners and wounding two other prisoners. This time he could be put to death.

It didn't look good. But Kirk wasn't worried. He didn't plan to be around for the trial.

The Plan

Mary Evans met Tim Kirk in August 1982, when she was given his **case.** She was a bright, successful, 27-year-old lawyer. But something happened while she was trying to defend Kirk that would change her life forever.

Since their first meeting, Evans had made 21 trips to the prison to prepare for Kirk's **murder** trial. They had been alone in the visitors' room only twice. The prison guards never noticed anything **unusual** about the visits.

But somehow Kirk had talked Evans into helping him escape. A week before the trial, they made their plans. Kirk asked Evans to bring some heavy tape and street clothes with her on the day of the escape. He also asked her to bring two guns.

Tim Kirk

No Turning Back

Soon after her last meeting with Kirk, Evans went to prison officials. She said, "I want a doctor to give Tim Kirk some tests. I need the results for his trial."

Officials set up the tests with Dr. Gary Salk. On March 31, 1983, three guards took Kirk to Dr. Salk's office. Mary Evans was waiting for them. She asked the guards to remove Kirk's handcuffs and leg irons during the tests. They agreed.

The tests lasted a couple of hours. When Kirk finished, Dr. Salk began to write up the results.

"Can I go out in the hall and have a smoke?" Kirk asked.

The doctor nodded. Kirk stepped out into the hall. Evans and the guards were waiting there. Evans reached into her purse and pulled out two guns. Calmly, she handed a gun to Kirk.

"All right, put your hands on your heads," Kirk told the guards.

The three guards obeyed. Kirk led them back into Dr. Salk's office. Evans ran to her car to get the tape and clothes. Then she returned to Dr. Salk's office.

In the office, Evans pointed her gun at Dr. Salk. He stared at her in **amazement.** But she just stared back. She didn't seem to care what he or anyone else thought.

A Heavy Price to Pay

Kirk kept his gun pointed at the four men. Evans cut long strips of tape and handed them to Kirk. He used the tape to tie up the four men. Then Evans cut the cord to the telephone. She waited while Kirk took off his prison uniform. He put on the clothes that she had brought.

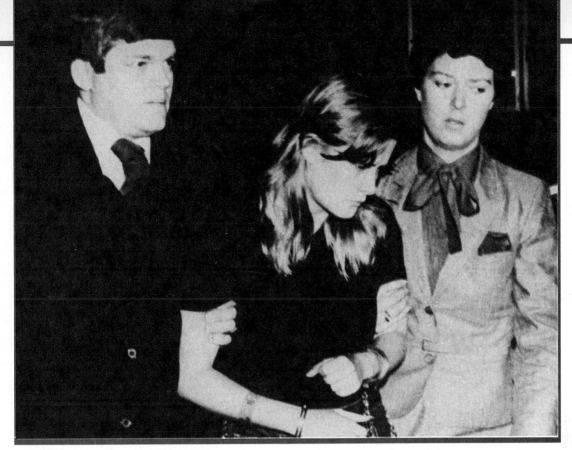

Officers lead Mary Evans to jail.

"Okay, let's go," Kirk said at last.

Evans did not **hesitate.** She knew she was giving up her family, her friends, and her work. But she didn't seem to care. She walked quickly out the door with Kirk. The two of them climbed into her car and drove away.

It took police five months to find Kirk and Evans. They had been living in Florida. In August, they were brought back to Tennessee to stand trial. Tim Kirk was given 40 extra years behind bars. Mary Evans was given three years for helping him escape. As the guards led her to prison, she showed no **regret.**

Even though the case was closed, it left many questions unanswered. How did Kirk talk Evans into helping him escape? Why was Evans willing to give up so much? No one understood why she had taken the law into her own hands.

Do You Remember?

■ In the blank, write the letter of the best ending for each sentence.

_____ 1. Mary Evans was a
     a. lawyer.   b. nurse.   c. teacher.

_____ 2. Tim Kirk was in prison for
     a. writing bad checks.
     b. armed robbery.
     c. kidnapping.

_____ 3. Tim Kirk was taken to Dr. Salk's office by
     a. guards.   b. his sister.   c. a judge.

_____ 4. Dr. Gary Salk gave Tim Kirk some
     a. guns.   b. sleeping pills.   c. tests.

_____ 5. Mary Evans and Tim Kirk were found in
     a. Tennessee.   b. Florida.   c. Arkansas.

Critical Thinking – Main Ideas

■ Underline the two most important ideas from the story.

1. Tim Kirk was 36 years old.

2. Tim Kirk convinced his lawyer to help him escape from prison.

3. Mary Evans surprised everyone by running off with Tim Kirk.

4. Tim Kirk asked Mary Evans to bring tape to Dr. Salk's office.

5. Dr. Gary Salk sometimes gave tests to prisoners.

Exploring Words

■ Choose the correct word from the box to complete each sentence.

unusual	case	armed robbery	amazement	regret
charges	trial	hesitate	murdered	lawyer

1. To _____ means to stop for a moment because of doubt.

2. If someone has been killed on purpose, that person has been _____.

3. To feel badly about something you have done is to feel _____.

4. Something that is not ordinary is _____.

5. If you have _____ brought against you, you have been accused of something.

6. To be surprised and full of wonder is to feel _____.

7. Using a gun to steal something is known as _____.

8. A court holds a _____ to decide if someone is guilty or not.

9. A person who represents someone in a court of law is a _____.

10. A _____ is a matter to be decided in a court of law.

Glossary

amazement, page 82
Amazement means great surprise.

angle, page 46
An angle is the slant or slope of something. The plane was coming in at a sharp angle.

anxiously, page 5
Anxiously means nervously.

armed robbery, page 80
Armed robbery means using a weapon to rob someone.

attempt, page 51
An attempt is a try.

attendant, page 58
An attendant is a person who helps or serves passengers.

attract, page 26
To attract means to bring something near.

audience, page 5
An audience is a group of people who watches or listens.

barbed, page 12
Barbed means having sharp points.

barbershop, page 52
A barbershop is a place where hair is cut.

barnacle, page 26
A barnacle is a small sea animal with a hard shell. It often fastens itself to the bottom of a ship.

bay, page 50
A bay is a body of water that is partly surrounded by land.

biscuit, page 25
In Britain, a biscuit is a cracker or cookie.

blast, page 19
To blast means to attack with words.

blend, page 67
Blend means to mix.

bolt, page 5
To bolt means to lock with a bar.

bomber, page 30
A bomber is a type of war plane that drops bombs.

border, page 12
A border is what separates two countries.

calm, page 38
If you feel calm, you feel peaceful. You are not excited or upset.

case, page 81
A case is a matter to be decided in a court of law.

channel, page 45
A radio station uses a channel to send messages to the people listening to it.

charge, page 80
If you are charged with robbery, it means you are accused of robbery.

chest, page 43

A chest is the part of a person's body between the neck and the stomach.

clue, page 75

A clue is something that helps to solve a mystery.

cockpit, page 59

The cockpit is the place in an airplane where the pilot sits.

column, page 18

A column is a long, straight row of people.

combat, page 8

Combat is fighting in a war.

Communist, page 73

A Communist believes most property should be owned by the state and shared by the people.

compass, page 10

A compass is a tool used to find directions.

concrete, page 52

Concrete is a hard material made of cement, sand, and water. The prison walls were made of concrete.

congratulations, page 33

Congratulations is what you say to people when you are happy with their good luck.

controls, page 43

The controls are used to start, stop, or keep an airplane in the air.

courage, page 63

If you are very brave, you have courage.

cramp, page 66

If a muscle cramps, it tightens painfully.

criminal, page 55

A criminal is someone who has broken the law.

crush, page 5

If something is crushed, it is squeezed painfully.

current, page 51

A current is flowing water.

cushion, page 32

To cushion means to soften.

daring, page 36

Daring means brave and willing to take chances.

deadly, page 69

If something is deadly, it can cause a person or animal to die.

death, page 5

Death means the end of life.

derail, page 38

If a train derails, it runs off the tracks.

desperate, page 46

Desperate means ready to take any chance.

discourage, page 11

To discourage means to lose hope.

entire, page 39

Entire means whole or complete. The entire family means the whole family.

experienced, page 43

A person who is experienced has done something many times.

fake, page 52

If something is fake, it is not real.

fearfully, page 5

Fearfully means filled with fear.

fir, page 32

A fir is a type of tree with needles. It is sometimes used as a Christmas tree.

galley, page 58

A galley is the kitchen in an airplane or ship.

gear, page 46

Gear is the equipment needed for a special job. The pilot lowered the plane's landing gear.

head, page 36

To head means to go in a certain direction.

height, page 77

Height is how high something is. We flew to a height of 8,500 feet.

hesitate, page 83

Hesitate means to stop for a moment because of doubt.

hijacking, page 59

A hijacking is the act of taking an airplane by force.

huddle, page 77

Huddle means to sit close together.

incredible, page 33

Incredible means hard to believe.

inflate, page 74

Inflate means to fill with air.

jammed, page 62

If something is jammed, it is stuck or locked into position.

jolt, page 39

A jolt is a sudden jerk.

lawyer, page 80

A lawyer's job is to represent someone in a court of law.

lieutenant, page 8

A lieutenant is an officer in the army.

line, page 9

A line is a group of soldiers side by side.

long, page 37

To long for something means to wish for it very much.

mainland, page 51

The mainland is the main part of a continent. The island was two miles from the mainland.

material, page 74

Material is cloth.

merchant, page 24

A merchant ship is one that carries goods to be sold.

microphone, page 44

A microphone is an instrument you speak into to send a message by radio.

mission, page 8

A mission is a special job to be done.

murder, page 81

Murder means killing someone on purpose.

mysteriously, page 5

Mysteriously means not able to be understood.

neighboring, page 68

Neighboring means nearby.

nuclear reactor, page 61

A nuclear reactor is part of a power plant that makes large amounts of energy and heat.

official, page 50

An official is a person who is in charge of something.

overwhelming, page 68

Overwhelming means too great to ignore.

panic, page 5

To panic means to have great fear.

paused, page 16

If you paused, you stopped or rested for a short time.

platform, page 73

A platform is a raised floor.

raft, page 20

A raft is a flat surface used to float on the water.

ration, page 18

To ration means to control the amount of something a person can have.

refugee, page 69

A refugee is a person who leaves home because his or her life is in danger.

regret, page 83

Regret is the feeling of being sorry.

rescue, page 20

Rescue means to save from danger.

roadblock, page 37

A roadblock is something put across a road to stop cars.

roam, page 69

Roam means to go from place to place.

rumble, page 66

Rumble means to make a deep sound.

runway, page 45

A runway is a strip of ground used for the landing and taking off of airplanes.

scan, page 30

To scan means to look carefully.

searchlight, page 30

A searchlight is a lamp used to send a bright beam of light in many directions.

sergeant, page 30

A sergeant is an officer in the army.

shark, page 26

A shark is a dangerous fish with tough skin and rows of sharp teeth.

shatter, page 30

When something shatters, it breaks into many pieces.

shipmate, page 25

Shipmates are people who sail on a ship together.

slippery, page 21

If something is slippery, it is smooth and wet and might cause someone to fall.

slump, page 43

If you slump in a chair, you are half sitting and half lying down.

spot, page 10

To spot means to see.

sprained, page 32

If you sprained your knee, it means you hurt it by twisting it.

steward, page 24

A steward is a person who takes care of the needs of passengers on a ship.

stun, page 3

To stun means to surprise greatly.

subject, page 73

A subject is an area that is thought about and discussed. They had many books on that subject.

submarine, page 24

A submarine is a ship that travels underwater.

succeed, page 2

To succeed means to do something that turns out well.

sue, page 60

If you are sued, you are taken to court by someone who wants money from you.

sunstroke, page 18

A sunstroke causes a person to faint from too much sun.

survive, page 24

Survive means to live through something dangerous.

survivor, page 67

A survivor is a person who lives through something dangerous.

suspicious, page 38

Suspicious means having the feeling that something is wrong.

taffeta, page 74

Taffeta is a shiny, silky cloth.

terrorist, page 58

A terrorist is a person who forces others to do what he or she wants.

throttle, page 39

The throttle is the lever that controls the speed of something.

torpedo, page 24

A torpedo is a cigar-shaped bomb. It is fired from a ship and travels underwater.

translator, page 67

A translator is a person who changes one language into another language. Translators help people who speak different languages talk to each other.

treat, page 21

To treat is to act in a certain way toward someone.

trial, page 80

If you are accused of a crime, you have a trial. The purpose of the trial is to decide if you are innocent or guilty.

unusual, page 81

If something is unusual, it is not ordinary or common.

vent, page 52

A vent is an opening through which air passes.

volt, page 12

A volt is a unit used to measure electricity.

vow, page 75

Vow means to promise.

wearily, page 61

Wearily means in a tired way.

will, page 17

Will is the power of the mind to decide and do something.

Chart Your Progress

Stories	Do You Remember?	Exploring Words	Critical Thinking	Express Yourself	Score
No Lock Could Hold Him			////		/20
Running for the Border				////	/22
Marching Out of Burma			////		/23
Alone on a Raft				////	/20
Tumbling Through the Sky			////		/20
Train Ride to Freedom				////	/23
Crash Landing!			////		/23
Prison Break!				////	/17
Hijacking!			////		/23
Survival in Cambodia				////	/22
Balloon Ride to Freedom			////		/20
Lawyer Turns Outlaw				////	/17

Finding Your Score
1. Count the number of correct answers you have for each activity.
2. Write these numbers in the boxes in the chart.
3. Ask your teacher to give you a score (maximum score 5) for **Express Yourself.**
4. Add up the numbers to get a final score.

Answer Key

No Lock Could Hold Him
Pages 2-7

Do You Remember? 1-a, 2-b, 3-c, 4-a, 5-a

Express Yourself: Answers will vary.

Exploring Words: 1-a, 2-c, 3-c, 4-a, 5-c, 6-b, 7-b, 8-a, 9-a, 10-c

Running for the Border
Pages 8-15

Do You Remember? 1-F, 2-F, 3-T, 4-F, 5-T, 6-T, 7-F, 8-T

Critical Thinking — Drawing Conclusions:
Answers may vary. Here are some examples.
1. he wanted to escape from the prison.
2. they should have been back within 24 hours.
3. they had to cut through the electric fence.
4. they realized the three men were trying to cross the border.

Exploring Words: Across: 2. volts, 5. discouraged, 7. combat, 9. mission
Down: 1. border, 3. lieutenant, 4. barbed, 6. spot, 7. compass, 8. line

Marching Out of Burma
Pages 16-23

Do You Remember? 1-F, 2-F, 3-T, 4-T, 5-F, 6-F, 7-T, 8-T

Express Yourself: Answers will vary.

Exploring Words: 1. paused, 2. column, 3. sunstroke, 4. slippery, 5. will, 6. blasted, 7. treated, 8. rationed, 9. rafts, 10. rescued

Alone on a Raft
Pages 24-29

Do You Remember? 1-b, 2-b, 3-a, 4-b, 5-c

Critical Thinking — Finding the Sequence:
5, 4, 1, 3, 2

Exploring Words: 1. submarine, 2. survive, 3. shipmates, 4. Barnacles, 5. merchant, 6. torpedo, 7. steward, 8. attract, 9. biscuits, 10. shark

Tumbling Through the Sky!
Pages 30-35

Do You Remember? 1-a, 2-c, 3-c, 4-a, 5-c

Express Yourself: Answers will vary.

Exploring Words: Across:
3. congratulations, 5. sprain, 8. bomber, 9. sergeant
Down: 1. incredible, 2. fir, 3. cushioned, 4. searchlights, 6. shattered, 7. scanned

Train Ride to Freedom
Pages 36-41

Do You Remember? 1-b, 2-c, 3-c, 4-b, 5-c

Critical Thinking — Fact or Opinion?
1-O, 2-F, 3-F, 4-O, 5-F, 6-O, 7-F, 8-O

Exploring Words: 1-c, 2-c, 3-b, 4-b, 5-a, 6-c, 7-a, 8-b, 9-c, 10-b

Crash Landing!
Pages 42-49

Do You Remember? 1-F, 2-T, 3-T, 4-F, 5-F, 6-T, 7-T, 8-F

Express Yourself: Answers will vary.

Exploring Words: 1. experienced, 2. chest, 3. slumped, 4. microphone, 5. channels, 6. desperate, 7. runway, 8. controls, 9. gear, 10. angle

Prison Break!
Pages 50-57

Do You Remember? 1-c, 2-b, 3-a, 4-c, 5-c

Critical Thinking — Main Ideas: 1, 5

Exploring Words: Across: 2. barbershop, 6. fake, 7. vent, 9. mainland, 10. currents
Down: 1. criminal, 3. attempts, 4. bay, 5. officials, 8. concrete

Hijacking!
Pages 58-65

Do You Remember? 1-F, 2-T, 3-T, 4-T, 5-F, 6-T, 7-F, 8-F

Express Yourself: Answers will vary.

Exploring Words: 1. cockpit, 2. attendant, 3. hijacking, 4. wearily, 5. terrorist, 6. galley, 7. courage, 8. nuclear reactor, 9. sued, 10. jammed

Survival in Cambodia
Pages 66-71

Do You Remember? 1-T, 2-T, 3-F, 4-T, 5-F, 6-F, 7-F, 8-T

Critical Thinking — Cause and Effect: Answers may vary. Here are some examples.
1. he was very hungry.
2. he knew the Khmer Rouge would kill him if they found out about it.
3. he had tried to steal rice.
4. he was afraid border guards would see him and kill him.

Exploring Words: 1-c, 2-b, 3-a, 4-a, 5-a, 6-c, 7-b, 8-a, 9-a, 10-c

Balloon Ride to Freedom
Pages 72-79

Do You Remember? 1-b, 2-b, 3-a, 4-a, 5-c

Express Yourself: Answers will vary.

Exploring Words: 1. Communists, 2. subject, 3. material, 4. inflate, 5. taffeta, 6. vowed, 7. height, 8. huddled, 9. platform, 10. clues

Lawyer Turns Outlaw
Pages 80-85

Do You Remember? 1-a, 2-b, 3-a, 4-c, 5-b

Critical Thinking — Main Ideas: 2, 3

Exploring Words: 1. hesitate, 2. murdered, 3. regret, 4. unusual, 5. charges, 6. amazement, 7. armed robbery, 8. trial, 9. lawyer, 10. case